STATE PROFILES

MINNESOTA

BY DEREK ZOBEL

BELLWETHER MEDIA • MINNEAPOLIS, MN

Blastoff! Discovery launches a new mission: reading to learn. Filled with facts and features, each book offers you an exciting new world to explore!

BLASTOFF! UNIVERSE

BLASTOFF! Beginners — GRADE K

BLASTOFF! READERS — GRADES 1-3

DISCOVERY — GRADE 4

This edition first published in 2022 by Bellwether Media, Inc.

No part of this publication may be reproduced in whole or in part without written permission of the publisher.
For information regarding permission, write to Bellwether Media, Inc.,
Attention: Permissions Department,
6012 Blue Circle Drive, Minnetonka, MN 55343.

Library of Congress Cataloging-in-Publication Data

Names: Zobel, Derek, 1983- author.
Title: Minnesota / by Derek Zobel.
Description: Minneapolis, MN : Bellwether Media, Inc., [2022] |
    Series: Blastoff! Discovery: State profiles | Includes bibliographical
    references and index. | Audience: Ages 7-13 | Audience: Grades
    4-6 | Summary: "Engaging images accompany information about
    Minnesota. The combination of high-interest subject matter and
    narrative text is intended for students in grades 3 through 8"–
    Provided by publisher.
Identifiers: LCCN 2021019689 (print) | LCCN 2021019690 (ebook)
    | ISBN 9781644873946 (library binding) | ISBN
    9781648341717 (ebook)
Subjects: LCSH: Minnesota–Juvenile literature.
Classification: LCC F606.3 .Z63 2022 (print) | LCC F606.3 (ebook)
    | DDC 977.6–dc23
LC record available at https://lccn.loc.gov/2021019689
LC ebook record available at https://lccn.loc.gov/2021019690

Editor: Colleen Sexton   Designer: Brittany McIntosh

Printed in the United States of America, North Mankato, MN.

TABLE OF CONTENTS

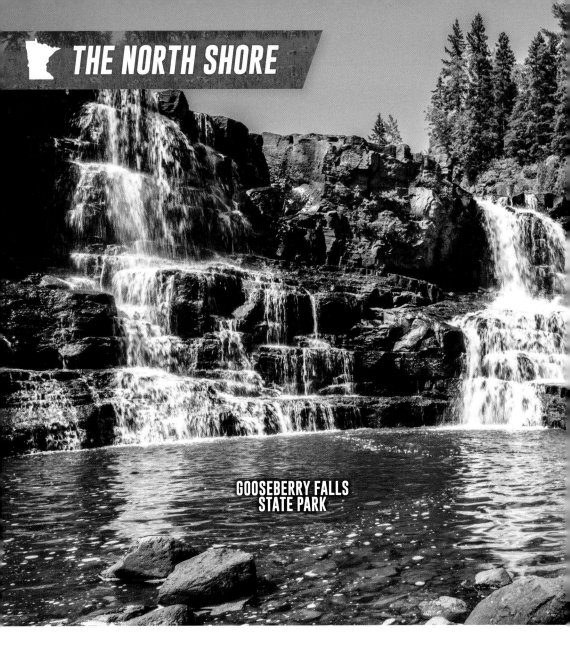

GOOSEBERRY FALLS
STATE PARK

A family is hiking on a sunny summer day in northern Minnesota. They begin at Gooseberry Falls State Park and trek to the waterfalls. Water spills over the upper, middle, and lower falls. The family wades into shallow pools of water. Soon the hikers leave the falls behind to continue north along the shore of Lake Superior.

BOUNDARY WATERS CANOE AREA

MALL OF AMERICA

MISSISSIPPI RIVER HEADWATERS

PAUL BUNYAN AND BABE THE BLUE OX

LIGHTING THE WAY

Storms can make the North Shore a dangerous shipping route. One storm in 1905 wrecked 29 ships. This loss led to the building of Split Rock Lighthouse in 1910.

Birds chirp in the forest as the family spots a deer. After several miles, they reach Split Rock Lighthouse State Park and follow the trail to the lake. Waves crash against the steep cliff where the old lighthouse stands. Welcome to Minnesota!

Minnesota is part of the **Upper Midwest** region of the United States. It shares a northern border with Canada. Lake Superior and Wisconsin meet Minnesota's eastern border. Iowa lies to the south. South Dakota and North Dakota form the western border. Minnesota covers a total of 86,936 square miles (225,163 square kilometers).

Most Minnesotans live in and around the Twin Cities in east-central Minnesota. These cities are the capital, Saint Paul, and the largest city, Minneapolis. Rochester and Duluth are other large cities in Minnesota.

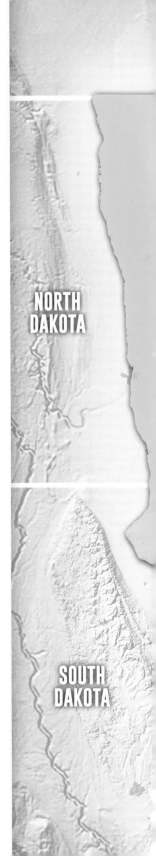

NORTH DAKOTA

SOUTH DAKOTA

CANADA

LAKE
SUPERIOR

DULUTH

MINNESOTA

MINNEAPOLIS

SAINT PAUL

WISCONSIN

ROCHESTER

N
W E
S

IOWA

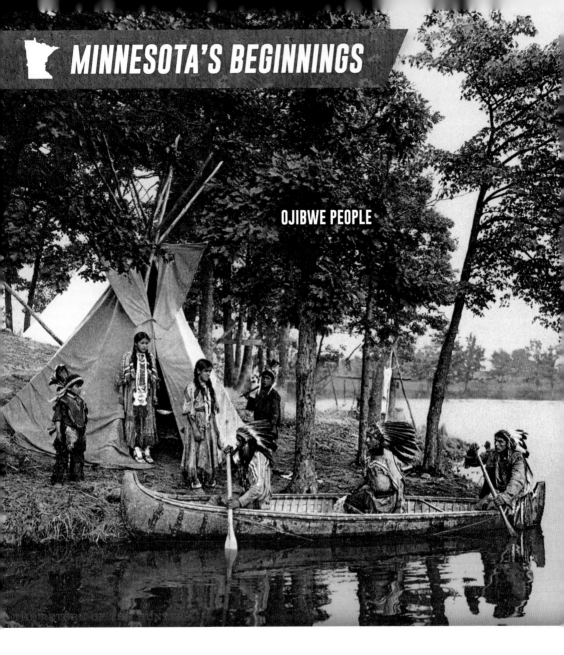

OJIBWE PEOPLE

The first people arrived in Minnesota around 12,000 years ago. The area eventually became home to the Dakota tribe. The Ojibwe entered Minnesota from the east several hundred years ago. They fought the Dakota and pushed them south.

French explorers came to Minnesota in the mid-1600s. Fur traders from other European countries soon followed. American **settlers** and **immigrants** arrived in the early 1800s after the **Louisiana Purchase**. Farmers and loggers cleared the land. This led to conflict with the Dakota and Ojibwe. The tribes were later forced off their homelands. In 1858, Minnesota joined the United States as the 32nd state.

NATIVE PEOPLES OF MINNESOTA

OJIBWE PEOPLE

- Original lands in northern Minnesota, mainly along Lake Superior
- More than 37,000 in Minnesota today
- Also called Chippewa and Anishinaabe

DAKOTA PEOPLE

- Original lands in central and southern Minnesota
- About 4,000 in Minnesota today
- Also called Sioux and Lakota

Minnesota is known as the Land of 10,000 Lakes. The largest within the state are Red Lake and Mille Lacs Lake. On the northeastern border lie the lakes and streams of the Boundary Waters wilderness area. Forests cover northern Minnesota and the mineral-rich Iron Range.

RED LAKE

IRON RANGE

MISSISSIPPI RIVER

MILLE LACS LAKE

MINNESOTA RIVER

N W+E S

Southeastern Minnesota features woodlands and **bluffs**. The **prairies** in the west and southwest are mostly farmland. The Mississippi and Minnesota Rivers are two of the state's many waterways.

MINNESOTA'S FUTURE: CLIMATE CHANGE

Minnesota is becoming warmer and wetter because of climate change. Residents are also experiencing stronger storms. These changes have led to more flooding and challenges in growing crops.

MISSISSIPPI RIVER
RED WING

MINNEHAHA FALLS
MINNEAPOLIS

SPRING
HIGH: 53°F (12°C)
LOW: 32°F (0°C)

SUMMER
HIGH: 78°F (26°C)
LOW: 56°F (13°C)

FALL
HIGH: 53°F (12°C)
LOW: 34°F (1°C)

WINTER
HIGH: 22°F (-6°C)
LOW: 4°F (-16°C)

°F = degrees Fahrenheit
°C = degrees Celsius

Minnesota has four seasons. Summers in Minnesota are hot and **humid**. Winters bring below-zero temperatures and heavy snowfall. Minnesotans must be prepared for blizzards in winter, floods in spring, and tornadoes in summer.

COMMON LOONS

Minnesota is home to many different kinds of animals. Owls, eagles, and other birds of prey patrol the skies looking for their next meal. Packs of wolves prowl through northern forests to hunt moose, deer, and smaller prey. They compete for food with black bears, lynx, and coyotes.

Beavers, loons, and muskrats build homes in Minnesota's many lakes and rivers. Walleye, bass, northern pike, and other fish swim in these waters. On the prairies, moles and ground squirrels hide from rattlesnakes and foxes.

THIRTEEN-LINED GROUND SQUIRREL

RED FOX

CANADA LYNX

MUSKRAT

QUITE THE HOWL

Wolves howl to communicate with each other. A howl can be as loud as a running lawn mower!

GRAY WOLF

Life Span: up to 13 years
Status: least concern

gray wolf range =

LEAST CONCERN	NEAR THREATENED	VULNERABLE	ENDANGERED	CRITICALLY ENDANGERED	EXTINCT IN THE WILD	EXTINCT

13

Minnesotans come from many backgrounds. Dakota and Ojibwe in the state may live on **reservations**, though many Ojibwe live around the Twin Cities. Many Minnesotans are **descendants** of European immigrants from Germany, Norway, Sweden, and Ireland. More recently, immigrants have arrived from Laos, Somalia, India, and Mexico.

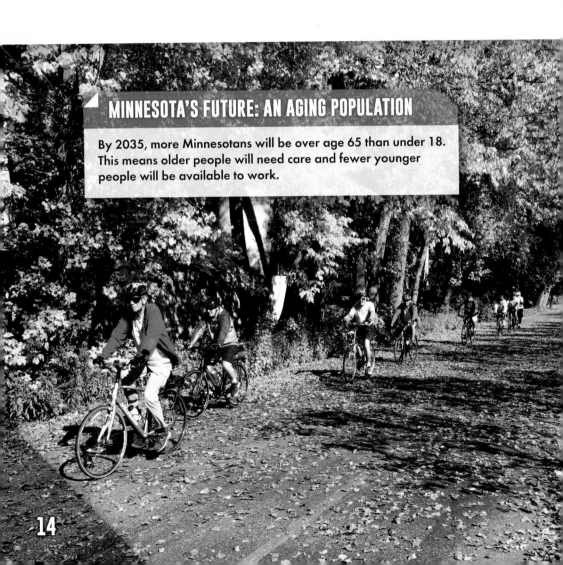

▶ MINNESOTA'S FUTURE: AN AGING POPULATION

By 2035, more Minnesotans will be over age 65 than under 18. This means older people will need care and fewer younger people will be available to work.

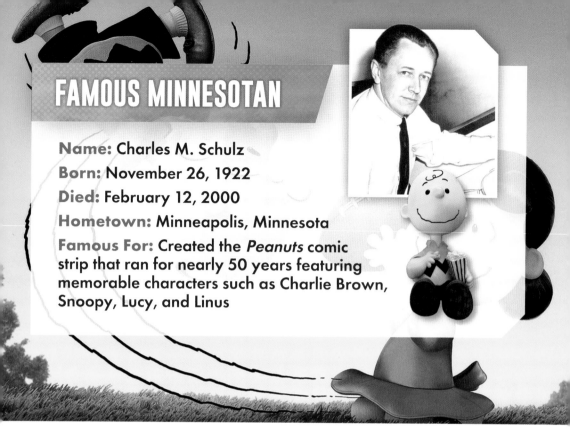

FAMOUS MINNESOTAN

Name: Charles M. Schulz
Born: November 26, 1922
Died: February 12, 2000
Hometown: Minneapolis, Minnesota
Famous For: Created the *Peanuts* comic strip that ran for nearly 50 years featuring memorable characters such as Charlie Brown, Snoopy, Lucy, and Linus

Almost three of every four Minnesotans live in and around cities. Most live in Minneapolis, Saint Paul, and the surrounding areas. **Rural** residents make their homes on farms and in small towns. They live mainly in western and northern Minnesota. The population of rural areas is shrinking as Minnesotans seek jobs in cities.

DOWNTOWN MINNEAPOLIS

ST. PAUL

MISSISSIPPI RIVER

Minneapolis and Saint Paul are known as the Twin Cities. The Mississippi River separates these two important cities. Saint Paul is the state capital. It began as a small settlement in 1838. Minneapolis was first settled in 1849. It is Minnesota's largest city in both area and population.

The Twin Cities are famous for their theaters, museums, and concert halls. Saint Paul is known for its historic **architecture**. Downtown Minneapolis is more modern. Lakes dot the city, earning it the nickname City of Lakes. Both cities use **skyways** to link buildings, keeping residents warm in the cold winters.

A STOLEN CAPITAL?

Early Minnesota leaders voted to move the capital to Saint Peter. This city lies southwest of Saint Paul along the Minnesota River. But one of the leaders stole the bill, and the capital was never moved!

SKYWAY
MINNEAPOLIS

Minnesota's many **natural resources** provided work for early immigrants. Miners dug up iron ore that cargo ships transported across the **Great Lakes**. Loggers floated timber from northern forests down the Mississippi River to lumber mills. Farmers brought wheat to grain **mills** in towns and cities.

CARGO CENTRAL

The Port of Duluth-Superior is the busiest port on the Great Lakes. It handles an average of 70 billion pounds (32 billion kilograms) of cargo every year!

Today, most Minnesotans have **service jobs** in health care, retail, and finance. Farmers grow soybeans, corn, and wheat. They also raise livestock. Factory workers produce medical devices, chemicals, and processed foods. Target, Best Buy, and 3M are a few of the major companies in the state. The world-famous Mayo Clinic is also based in Minnesota.

INVENTED IN MINNESOTA

ROLLERBLADES
Date Invented: 1980
Inventors: Scott and Brennan Olson

NERF BALL
Date Invented: 1969
Inventor: Reyn Guyer

SCOTCH TAPE
Date Invented: 1930
Inventor: Richard Drew (3M employee)

HONEYCRISP APPLE
Date Invented: 1991 (released)
Inventors: University of Minnesota

TATER TOT HOT DISH

Classic Minnesota foods include wild rice, walleye, and hot dish. Wild rice grows in the state's lakes and rivers. Cooks often use it to make wild rice soup. Walleye caught in the state's many lakes is served baked, deep fried, or in sandwiches. A hot dish combines meat, potatoes, vegetables, and canned soup into one baked meal.

DON'T PHO-GET ABOUT IT!

Immigrants from eastern Asia brought *pho* to Minnesota. This hearty soup features broth, rice noodles, meat, peppers, and bean sprouts.

The state's early immigrants brought many of the **traditional** foods that Minnesotans enjoy. **Scandinavians** introduced pancake-like *lefse* and Swedish meatballs. Germans brought sausages and thin, battered *schnitzels* to Minnesota. Italian immigrants popularized porketta on the Iron Range in northern Minnesota.

LEFSE

SCHNITZEL

CREAMY WILD RICE SOUP

6 SERVINGS

Have an adult help you make this recipe!

INGREDIENTS

1/3 cup finely chopped onion
6 tablespoons butter
1/2 cup flour
3 cups chicken broth
2 cups cooked wild rice
1/2 cup grated carrots

1 cup cooked chicken breast, cut into pieces
3 tablespoons slivered almonds
1/2 teaspoon salt
1 cup half and half

DIRECTIONS

1. In a large saucepan, melt the butter over medium heat.

2. Add the onions to the butter, and cook for a few minutes.

3. Add the flour, stirring constantly until the mixture is bubbly.

4. Slowly stir in the broth.

5. Add the wild rice, carrots, chicken, almonds, and salt.

6. Simmer for 5 minutes.

7. Add the half and half. Heat through.

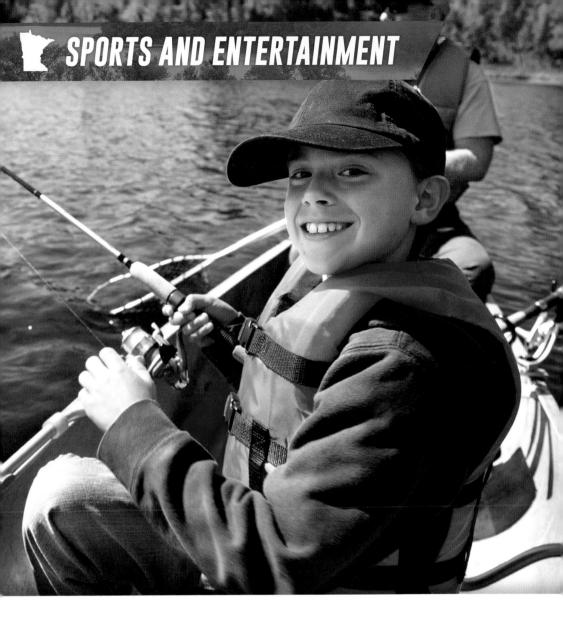

Minnesotans enjoy the outdoors all year long. They bike, hike, and camp in the state's many parks. In warm weather, people head to lakes and rivers to fish, swim, and boat. In the winter, residents enjoy skiing, snowmobiling, hockey, and ice fishing. Minnesotans cheer for professional baseball, hockey, football, soccer, and basketball teams.

Minnesota is a hot spot for the arts. Residents enjoy music, fine art, and theater year-round. Minneapolis has the Guthrie Theater, the Walker Art Center, and First Avenue. Saint Paul features the Fitzgerald Theater and the Ordway Center, home to the Saint Paul Chamber Orchestra.

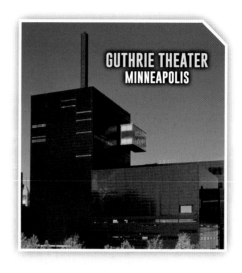

GUTHRIE THEATER
MINNEAPOLIS

NOTABLE SPORTS TEAM

Minnesota Lynx
Sport: Women's National Basketball Association
Started: 1999
Place of Play: Target Center

JOHN BEARGREASE
SLED DOG MARATHON
DULUTH

Minnesotans celebrate events all year. The annual Saint Paul Winter Carnival features ice palaces, ice sculpture contests, and parades. Up north, the John Beargrease Sled Dog Marathon challenges racers. They compete on a tough course that stretches for almost 300 miles (483 kilometers)!

TALL TALES

Minnesotans remember their logging history through the folklore of Paul Bunyan and his blue ox, Babe. The city of Akeley celebrates these legends every year. It holds fishing contests, a parade, and a Paul Bunyan look-alike contest.

Millions of people head to the Minnesota State Fair in the summer. They eat sweet corn, fried cheese curds, and pronto pups. Exhibits feature farm animals, butter sculptures, and farm equipment. Businesses display new products, and local artists show off their artwork. The State Fair is a great way to celebrate all that Minnesota has to offer!

FRIED CHEESE CURDS

MINNESOTA STATE FAIR

1669

French fur traders enter Minnesota

1820

Construction begins on Fort Snelling where the Minnesota River and Mississippi River meet

1803

The Louisiana Purchase makes some of Minnesota part of the United States

1745

The Ojibwe defeat the Dakota and claim northern and eastern Minnesota

1992

The Mall of America opens
in Bloomington, Minnesota

2020

The death of George Floyd
sparks protests against
police brutality and racism in
Minneapolis, Saint Paul, and
cities across the country

1858

Minnesota becomes
the 32nd state

1862

The Dakota War ends with
the defeat of the Dakota
by the United States

2007

The Interstate 35W bridge over
the Mississippi River collapses

Nickname: The North Star State

Motto: *L'Etoile du Nord* (Star of the North)

Date of Statehood: May 11, 1858 (the 32nd state)

Capital City: Saint Paul ★

Other Major Cities: Minneapolis, Duluth, Rochester, Bloomington

Area: 86,936 square miles (225,163 square kilometers); Minnesota is the 12th largest state.

Population

5,706,494 (2020)

STATE FLAG

Adopted in 1957, the state flag of Minnesota features the state seal on a royal blue background. On the seal, a wreath of lady's slippers, the state flower, circles a farmer plowing his field and a Native American man on horseback. The state motto appears on a banner above them. The white ring around the seal has 19 stars, symbolizing that Minnesota was the 19th state to join the union after the 13 original colonies.

INDUSTRY

JOBS

- MANUFACTURING **9%**
- FARMING AND NATURAL RESOURCES **3%**
- GOVERNMENT **11%**
- SERVICES **77%**

Main Exports

 soybeans

 turkeys

 electronics

 medical products

 iron ore

 clean energy products

Natural Resources
ore, lumber, water, soil, stone

GOVERNMENT

10 ELECTORAL VOTES

Federal Government
8 REPRESENTATIVES | **2** SENATORS

 USA

 MN

State Government
134 REPRESENTATIVES | **67** SENATORS

STATE SYMBOLS

STATE BIRD
COMMON LOON

STATE FISH
WALLEYE

STATE FLOWER
PINK AND WHITE LADY'S SLIPPER

STATE TREE
RED PINE

29

GLOSSARY

architecture—the design of buildings and other structures

bluffs—steep cliffs that often overlook a body of water

descendants—people related to a person or group of people who lived at an earlier time

Great Lakes—large freshwater lakes on the border between Canada and the United States; the Great Lakes are Superior, Michigan, Ontario, Erie, and Huron.

humid—having a lot of moisture in the air

immigrants—people who move to a new country

Louisiana Purchase—a deal made between France and the United States; it gave the United States 828,000 square miles (2,144,510 square kilometers) of land west of the Mississippi River.

mills—buildings with machines for processing materials; mills produce materials such as lumber and flour.

natural resources—materials in the earth that are taken out and used to make products or fuel

prairies—large, open areas of grassland

reservations—areas of land that are controlled by Native American tribes

rural—related to the countryside

Scandinavians—people from the countries of Denmark, Norway, and Sweden

service jobs—jobs that perform tasks for people or businesses

settlers—people who move to live in a new, undeveloped region

skyways—series of enclosed walkways that connect buildings

traditional—related to customs, ideas, or beliefs handed down from one generation to the next

Upper Midwest—a region of the United States that includes Minnesota, Wisconsin, Michigan, Iowa, North Dakota, and South Dakota

AT THE LIBRARY

Casanova, Mary. *Wolf Shadows*. Minneapolis, Minn.: University of Minnesota Press, 2013.

Heinrichs, Ann. *Minnesota*. Mankato, Minn.: Child's World, 2017.

Kelley, K.C. *Minnesota Twins: Stars, Stats, History, and More!* Mankato, Minn.: Child's World, 2019.

ON THE WEB

FACTSURFER

Factsurfer.com gives you a safe, fun way to find more information.

1. Go to www.factsurfer.com.

2. Enter "Minnesota" into the search box and click 🔍.

3. Select your book cover to see a list of related content.

INDEX